808

CONVERSATION STARTERS for COUPLES

Spark Curious Chats During Dinner Time, Date Night or at Any Moment

ROBIN WESTEN

D0594697

Published in the United States by:
Ulysses Press
P.O. Box 3440
Berkeley, CA 94703
www.ulyssespress.com

ISBN: 978-1-61243-647-0
Library of Congress Control Number: 2016950666

Printed in Canada by Marquis Book Printing
10 9 8 7 6 5 4 3 2 1

Acquisitions editor: Bridget Thoreson
Managing editor: Claire Chun
Project editor: Kourtney Joy
Editor: Lauren Harrison
Proofreader: Shayna Keyles
Cover design: Rebecca Lown
Interior design: what!design @ whatweb.com
Images: plate © Djem/shutterstock.com; couple © Oksana Petrova/
    shutterstock.com; fireworks © rungrote/shutterstock.com

Distributed by Publishers Group West

"Ask the right questions, and the answers
will always reveal themselves."

—Oprah Winfrey

INTRODUCTION

Communication seems to be easier than ever. There's no short-age of options, from texting and email to Snapchat, Facebook, and Instagram. But this is the reality: when it comes to digging deeper and getting to the heart and soul of another being, well, we're pretty out of practice. How often have you sat across from your partner and heard the same old, same old? Or maybe you're the one asking the superficial and routine questions: How was your day? How do you feel? What do you want for dinner? What should we watch?

Sound familiar? Maybe too familiar? It's no wonder most of us have tuned out, and—sadly—sometimes turned off.

That's why I've written *808 Conversations Starters for Couples*. The questions offered on the following pages will help partners to dig deeper, unlock secrets, reveal passions, engage desires, and ultimately gain trust and intimacy.

Just imagine how a relationship can grow by learning something new about the person you've known for only a few weeks or for even decades. That's the power of thought-provoking, open-ended questions. They get us to dig deep, examine our motives, review our personal histories, crack our hearts open, and answer with honesty and—if we're even luckier—revelation.

But that's only half the picture. The other place to put your attention is in the arena of listening. You'll need to be fully present. Nobody wants to speak if the person on the receiving end is distracted, dismissive, or unresponsive. The truth is, listening is as powerful as asking. That's why before you begin this endeavor, vow to stay receptive and respectful. No answer should be dissed or denied. If you have doubts about the response, allow yourself to follow through, but from a place of curiosity and caring. With this in mind, prepare yourself to reach a new level of trust and loving with your partner. And who doesn't want that?

808

CONVERSATION
STARTERS

Let's say you're getting a tattoo inked in a prominent place. What does it look like?

You can have one wish granted. What is it?

Mini Quiz

You're dying for a bowl of breakfast cereal, but after pouring it out, you discover there's no milk. What to do?

a) Eat it dry and crunchy.

b) Go to the store for milk.

c) Pour it back in the box and stop off for breakfast somewhere.

If your clothes send a message about who you are, what are yours saying?

⸺ ⭐

How would you describe your relationship with your mother? And your father?

⸺ ⭐

If you could invite any living person to share a private spa weekend with you, who would it be and why?

Mini Quiz

For you, having two relationships going on at once would be:

a) Out of the question.

b) Confusing. You'd feel emotionally torn and drained.

c) Cool, as long as everyone felt comfortable with the situation.

Is fame something you want? If yes, how would you like to be known? If no, why not?

Who's your BFF? What are his or her qualities?

You open your door and find a super-cute kitten sitting on the welcome mat. What do you do?

⭐

Describe your best night ever.

⭐

You win a plane ticket to go anywhere in the world. Where do you want to land? What makes it so appealing?

⭐

Which actor gets major props from you? Why?

What did you write in your most embarrassing text (or email)?

Heavy alert: How do you want to be remembered after you die?

Mini Quiz

If you could add a room onto your home, would it be a:

a) Greenhouse, with roses, orchids, and other plants that grow all year round.

b) Giant bathroom, complete with enormous tub, multi-headed shower, and a steam room or sauna.

c) Gym, with a treadmill, weights, stationary cycle, and yoga area.

Mini Quiz

Which turns you on the most?

a) Super smarts

b) Sense of humor

c) Strong character

Which do you enjoy more,
giving or receiving? Why?

Describe the selfie you would love to take.

Can you share your most humiliating
childhood memory?

What do you respect most
about your partner?

What do you like least?

Do it! Belt out lyrics to your favorite song.

Mini Quiz

Which female newscaster would you want to
interview you?:

a) Diane Sawyer

b) Katie Couric

c) Meghan Kelly

When was the last time you broke down and had a real weep fest? What was it about?

⭐

What do you most regret in your life?

⭐

Name five things in your life that fill you with gratitude.

⭐

Do it! Ask your partner to help solve a problem you're having with a colleague or friend.

What are the top-six must-dos on your bucket list?

———— ★

If you were hoping for a promotion but a coworker got it instead, what would you do?

———— ★

Mini Quiz

If you chose a piece of candy from a box of chocolates, took a nibble, and didn't like it, would you:

a) Put it back and choose another one.

b) Throw it away and count your blessings that you saved the unappetizing calories.

c) Keep eating until you find one that tastes delish.

Mini Quiz

Which of these is the furthest from your comfort zone?

a) Leading a 6 a.m. yoga rave for a thousand yogis.

b) Accompanying two dozen toddlers on their preschool field trip.

c) Catering a brunch for 25 top chefs.

What's the most important piece of advice you ever received?

If you inherited $500,000, what would you do with it?

What does "unconditional love" mean to you?

Tell me about a time you lost something that was really valuable to you. What did you tell yourself to get over it? Or are you still feeling bad about your loss?

Mini Quiz

A friend's partner flirts with you. You consider this:

a) A compliment.

b) Possible trouble ahead.

c) The end of a friendship.

Why do you think so many bad
things happen in our world?

— ★

Which super hero would you
want to be? Describe his or her
power and why you desire it.

— ★

Why do you think you were born?

— ★

Name three things about life
you're certain about.

If you had to slip into a time machine
that only went backward, what year
would you go to and why?

Do you believe in ghosts? Why or why not?

Can you name at least five things
we share in common?

If you could hurt someone's reputation online,
where would you aim your poison arrow?

What's the most erotic dream you ever had?

⭐

Do it! Stare into each other's eyes
silently for at least three minutes.

⭐

If you had to either never binge watch TV
again or never set foot in a movie theater,
which would you choose to give up?

⭐

What's your hugest worry?

Mini Quiz

When you encounter an obstacle, you're most likely to:

a) Weigh whether you're chasing the right goal.

b) Decide it's best to change your approach.

c) Stay on course and work harder to solve the problem.

Do you feel like you're the same person you were ten years ago? In what ways are you the same? In what ways are you different?

If you could change a decision you made, what would it be?

Do it! Cuddle silently for five minutes.

★

What animal do you most resemble
when you're having sex?

★

Would you rather live in a very messy
and relaxed house or an uncluttered
and divinely decorated one?

★

What's your best time of day and what
are you usually doing during it?

Which statement best reflects your feelings about physical attraction?

a) It can be turned on and off like a faucet.

b) It's pure, uncontrollable magnetism.

c) It often requires careful cultivation.

What would be the worst job in the world for you and what makes it so wrong?

Is there anything that someone can say in this moment to make you feel better about yourself?

Do you believe in miracles?
Why or why not?

Has something good happened to a
friend and instead of feeling happy
for him or her you felt envious? What
do you think that was about?

Do you believe reincarnation is
for real? Why or why not?

What was a time in your life when
your self-esteem was lower than a
blade of freshly mowed grass?

Mini Quiz

At parties, your favorite thing to do is:

a) Hang with lots of different people.

b) Have an intimate one-on-one conversation.

c) Happily sit back by yourself and observe.

Do you get to airports really early for a flight or take your chances and guesstimate the least amount of waiting time? What's your reasoning?

Do you believe in soul mates, two people destined to be together?

Mini Quiz

Which of these statements most closely speaks your truth?

a) When one door closes, another opens.

b) You can't open the door without the golden key—and not everyone has it.

c) Some doors are better left locked.

If you knew you were going to die in a year, what would you be doing differently?

Have you ever been scammed? If so, how'd it go down? If not, how'd you suss it out?

Do you believe in love at first sight?

Do you have an enemy? What caused
the rift? And do you have regrets
about the way it was handled?

Do it! Sit across from one another,
close eyes, touch foreheads, and take
twenty deep breaths in unison.

Do you think animals are more
loving than people?

Are you comfortable with public display
of affection (PDA)? What's cool but
what's way too embarrassing?

— ★

Are you still in touch with your
exes? If not, why not?

— ★

Do you think happiness can be bought?

— ★

What would outrage you so much you would
take to the streets to protest? Or if you've
already done so, what was the cause?

Mini Quiz

Do you think true happiness is:

a) Something we have to work at to achieve.

b) Why we're alive.

c) An illusion.

If you had a free hour, what would
you probably do with it?

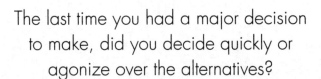

The last time you had a major decision
to make, did you decide quickly or
agonize over the alternatives?

Do you believe in fate or do you
think we create our future?

Would you rather see a thriller flick, romantic
comedy, or action movie? What do you
consider a classic film in your favorite
genre? Where did you see it? How did
you react during and after viewing?

What's your favorite season and
what do you like best about it?

Would you rather diet or work out?

Do you consider yourself more
of an introvert or extrovert?

—— ★

If you found a wallet with cash and
credit cards someone had left in a taxi
you're in, what would you do?

—— ★

What do you consider a total
no-no in a relationship?

—— ★

Do it! Whisper a sweet or sexy
sentiment into your partner's ear.

Are you an animal lover? Or do you
feel ambivalent about them?

Would you rather spend the afternoon
walking through the countryside
or the streets of Paris? Why?

Mini Quiz

If your horoscope suggested you avoid making
important decisions today, you would:

a) Put them off until tomorrow.

b) Ponder those decisions a little more carefully.

c) Ignore the warning.

When was the last time you told a lie? How come you felt the need to be deceitful?

When did you lose your virginity?
Was it a good experience, not so hot,
or something you'd rather forget?

Fourth of July, Christmas, Thanksgiving,
Valentine's Day—which is your favorite,
and what do you dig most about it?

Has your taste in music changed over
the years? What did you enjoy in the
past and what are you into now?

Mini Quiz

Let's say you run into your sister's husband arm-in-arm with another woman. You:

a) Phone your sister pronto!

b) Pull him aside and ask what the heck is going on!

c) Stay out of it.

How do you roll? Super planner or sucker for spontaneity?

Do you consider yourself religious, spiritual, or a non-believer? Has it always been this way? If not, what changed your belief system?

What do you think about porn?

Do it! Blindfold your partner and lead him or her around the house using just these verbal instructions: forward, back, left, right, go, stop.

Who have you lost touch with that you think about fairly regularly?

When you need help or advice, whom are you likely to ask?

Who's the luckiest person
you know and why?

★

Would you say you usually trust
your gut reaction or are you more
likely to use your intellect?

★

What's the weirdest photo you've
ever snapped with your phone?
Did you delete or post it?

★

Bloody hell! Are you into vampire
movies? Why or why not?

What did you buy online
that you really regret?

What's your take on gluten-free
diets? For real or all hype?

What are the six smartphone apps
you just can't do without?

What do you think about those whopper
Wall Street bonuses? Should there
be a cap on them or do you think
capitalism should be free to fly?

Mini Quiz

If you were suddenly a billionaire and swamped with requests for donations, what would you do?

a) Pick one favorite charity and gladly write a big, fat check.

b) Set up a foundation so others can also contribute.

c) Make anonymous donations to several different charities.

Do you rely on online reviews before making reservations at a hotel or restaurant or before buying a product? Why or why not?

Do it! Give your partner a hand massage.

If an energy company were planning on building a wind farm on property with a pristine view, would you be for or against it?

★

Would you say you are more cautious than carefree? For example, do you back up your computer files?

★

What about juicing? A good idea or bogus? What makes you come to this conclusion?

★

Have you ever been cyber-stalked? Or have you ever cyber-stalked someone else?

Let's say you're disconnected electronically. How long do you think you could go before freaking out and searching for a place that has a connection?

Do you believe there's power in prayer? Why or why not?

Imagine our world were run by women. How would it be different than it is today?

If you were to add one more commandment to the list of ten, what would it be?

Can you think of a cause that
would be worth dying for?

Have you ever stolen? Describe one incident.

Is there such a thing as too
many tattoos or piercings?

Do you think pot should be
legalized? Why or why not?

If you ran into a celebrity, would you ask for a selfie with them? If yes, would you post it somewhere? If not, what's your reasoning for not making the request?

Where do you like to people watch?

Mini Quiz

If you had a great idea but others resisted it, would you:

a) Offer another equally cool idea.

b) Just go along with the group.

c) Figure out a way to reframe your same idea.

What's something you really enjoyed doing as a kid but haven't done in years?

Do it! Put on your favorite slow tune and dance in each other's arms.

What object in your childhood bedroom do you wish you had now?

Do you have any desire to climb Mt. Everest? What do you imagine would be your greatest challenge?

What is the most powerful lesson
your mother taught you?

★

How often do you look at your email
and texts? Do you check, for example,
as soon as you wake up? Would you
like to stop checking so often?

★

How do you feel about all the surveillance
cameras in public spaces?

★

Do you think the earth is doomed?
What are some ways you do and
don't try to protect the environment?

Do you check food labels? What do you look for first: Calories? Carbs? Organic? GMO? If you're not concerned, what's your food philosophy?

What's the one question you're hoping won't be asked? What are you dying to talk about instead?

What are your qualifications?

Do you think you're a better judge of character or beauty?
What are your qualifications?

Do it! Take the trust fall. Stand up tall and stretch your arms out in front of you. Your partner is behind ready to catch you when you fall backward.

★

When no one else is around, what kind of music do you put on?

★

What saying would you put on a T-shirt?

★

Has the threat of terrorism ever kept you from traveling to another city or country or from going to a public event?

Most of us have a phobia of some kind.
What's yours and how do you deal with it?

⭐

Which actor would you love
to play opposite you?

⭐

Mini Quiz

In family photos are you usually:

a) Not there, since you're the one taking the
picture.

b) Wherever there's an open spot.

c) Smiling center stage.

How do you feel about the expression,
"It's better to have loved and lost
than never to have loved at all"?

Would you sing karaoke? What
song would be your first choice?

If your good friend were acting cruelly to her
partner, would you intervene? What if your
friend's partner was disrespecting your friend?

Do you believe love conquers all?

If there were one thing you could improve about yourself to make you a better friend, what would it be?

⸻ ☆

Would you say you had a pretty easygoing childhood?

⸻ ☆

If your beloved pet was sick and a treatment (which might, or might not, save him) would mean you had to borrow $5,000 dollars, would you do it? Or let him go? What's your reasoning?

Do you feel like you have a "calling" or are you open to going in wildly different directions?

Do it! Walk down the street hand-in-hand.

Mini Quiz

An ex who lives 3,000 miles away phones to say he or she is in town and would like to meet for lunch. Suddenly you feel the old passion return. You:

a) Meet in some out-of-the-way dive bar and let the heat rise.

b) Douse yourself with cold water and decline.

c) Agree to meet but keep it chill to the max.

What's the greatest gift anyone
could give you?

★

What would be the title of
your autobiography?

★

What is the biggest misunderstanding
you had with a friend and what was
done (or not done) to clear it up?

★

If you could activate any object just with
your voice, which one would it be?

Has a child ever taught you a
lesson you've never forgotten?

How honest would you be (or have you
been) when it comes to an online dating
profile? What little white lies have you told?

If you were only allowed to make one
call for help, who would you call?

What was the most memorable dare
you ever took? Do you have regrets?
Or are you grateful you did it?

What was the best New Year's
Eve celebration you ever had?

— ☆

What are five things you could do
that would improve your life?

— ☆

Would you live your life in a different
way if you didn't feel responsible
to others? In what ways?

— ☆

Which late-night talk show
would you love to be on?

Which family member do you most resemble in temperament? In looks? In special talents or interests?

⭐

Which *Jeopardy!* category would you choose first? Which would you try to avoid?

⭐

Mini Quiz

If your partner isn't responding to your hot advances, do you:

a) Try a different turn-on like a massage or a sexy movie.

b) Probably just feel rejected and hurt.

c) Assume your partner must be distracted or tired.

What is your strangest possession?
When did you get it? Would you sell it if
someone offered you twice its value?

⎯⎯ ⭐

Looking ahead to the next ten years, what
three goals would you like to achieve?

⎯⎯ ⭐

How important are other people
when it comes to your happiness?

⎯⎯ ⭐

Can you describe a place you used to go
or hide in when you were a kid? How often
did you go there? Why did you choose it?

What's the funniest comedy you've
ever seen? Can you recall one
or two hilarious scenes?

What do you obsess over?

What's a guilty pleasure you only
do when you're alone?

Do it! Hug and hold tight.

What do you remember most
about your first kiss?

Who are five people, dead or alive,
that you think are totally brilliant?

What's the wackiest thing you've ever done?

Did you ever lie about what you did
for a living, or where you grew up,
or where you went to school?

Do you think you could ever follow a guru? If yes, why? If not, how come?

★

What would be the plot to a TV sitcom that depicted your daily life?

★

What are your most annoying habits?

★

Do you believe less is more?

What part of your life do you consider "on hold," and what needs to happen to change your situation?

Can you name five people you would choose to live on an island with you? Why did you pick them?

What are three things that you see in the world around you that you find depressing?

What are three things that you see in the world around you that you find depressing?

Do you remember the worst rejection you ever felt? What happened?

Mini Quiz

You're visiting Italy but can't speak the language.
What do you do?

a) Resort to sign language.

b) Speak in clear, concise English.

c) Use a foreign language app.

What chore do you put off most frequently?

Have you ever walked out of a
movie or a concert? Why?

What health habit do you wish
you could develop?

How has getting older changed you?

What's the worst thing an ex
has ever done to you?

Did you ever make a fashion faux pas and
dress wildly inappropriately for an event?

Mini Quiz

If you witnessed a robbery on the street, would you:

a) Try to help the victim.

b) Get out of the way quickly.

c) Call 911.

What do you think would happen if you had to spend two days and two nights alone in a windowless room?

What beliefs would you defend to the end?

Is there something you wish you started early in life, such as learning to play a musical instrument or practicing a particular sport?

★

How often have you madly and truly fallen in love? And why wasn't it forever?

★

What's your idea of hot foreplay?

★

Have you ever had a dream that predicted the future?

How do you think the planet will look twenty-five years from now?

⭐

What kinds of thoughts could wake you from a deep sleep?

⭐

Would you create a clone of yourself? If your answer is yes, why? If your answer is no, why not?

⭐

Have you ever had a déjà vu experience? Can you describe it?

How did you first learn about "the birds and the bees"?

⭐

Do you have a memory of your parents totally embarrassing you in front of friends? What happened?

⭐

Mini Quiz

When making plans for the day, you tend to:

a) Go with the flow.

b) Make a list and try to stick to it.

c) Reprioritize throughout the day and often reconsider plans.

Would you like to know if you're
at risk for a particular illness even if
there were no treatment for it?

Would you rather live nearer to or
farther away from your parents?
What's your reasoning?

If you had long-time plans arranged
with a friend but something came up
unexpectedly and you had to break your
date, how would you deal with it?

If an ATM gave you extra cash, how likely is it that you would report it to the bank?

Do it! Cook a meal together.

Are you more of a listener than a talker? Or is it the other way around? Do you think you would benefit by assuming a different dynamic?

What sexual role-plays would turn you on the most?

Can you tell if someone is lying
to you? What clues do you look
for to detect dishonesty?

⭐

Can you define the word "mercy"?

⭐

What is the most heroic thing
you've ever done?

⭐

Do it! Collaborate on an easy art project.

In what ways do you step up to help make your partner's life easier? Do you think you should do more? Or do you think you're doing more than your share?

— ⭐

What would you do if you bumped into your doppelganger on the street?

— ⭐

Can a person be too rich?

— ⭐

Would you rather be a really well-known celebrity or unknown but responsible for saving dozens of lives?

What would be the hardest thing
to turn down even though you
know it's not good for you?

⭐

How and where do you like
being touched the most?

⭐

Have you ever witnessed what appeared
to be a supernatural event?

⭐

What do you think are the best reasons
for getting married? The worst?

How did your mom and dad meet?

What object do you still regret losing
either because of its material value
or for sentimental reasons?

What does your ideal home look like?

What do you think are five secrets to
a long, healthy, and happy life?

Can you talk about a superstition
that you sort of believe in?

Mini Quiz

If you reach a two-way stop sign at the same time as another driver, are you more likely to:

a) Wait and let the other car go.

b) Obey the rules of the road and yield appropriately.

c) Try to go through first.

If you owned a restaurant what would you call it and what would its specialty be?

Do it! Get in a steamy shower together.

If you believed that being frozen after you died would give you the chance to be brought back to life, but it costs your entire fortune and would leave no money for your heirs, would you do it?

If folks knew the real you—your secret weaknesses, fears, and feelings—would their opinion of you change drastically, a little bit, or not at all? What do you think would freak them out the most?

Which politician do you admire the most and why?

How do you approach thunder and lightning storms? With excitement or trepidation?

★

Would you join a medical study for a treatment that might lengthen your life even though doctors admit they aren't sure of its side effects?

★

What do you own that under no circumstances—no way—would you ever agree to loan or share?

★

What are three things that would definitely trigger your anger?

Do you have memories of your grandparents?

When you were a kid, what did you do
that got you into the worst trouble?

If you were a master builder,
what would you create?

How would you describe the universe?
Does it have a beginning and an end?

How often do you go to fast-food restaurants?

If you could get rid of one evil in this world, which would you choose and why?

———⭐

Do it! Send each other hot texts—
five words or fewer.

———⭐

What was your mother's
most annoying habit?

———⭐

When would you be likely to drink too much?

Have you learned something about your partner over the last three months that you didn't know before? What was it?

If your partner were sad, what would you do to turn the mood around?

If you accidentally dropped your partner's toothbrush in the toilet, retrieved it, and then cleaned it like crazy, would you admit what happened?

What's the dumbest thing you ever bought? Did you return it?

Recall the most recent time you apologized.
What happened? Was your apology
sincere or were you just trying to move on?

How did you meet your best friend?

What bums you out the most about politics?

Which comedian always cracks you up?
Do you remember part of the routine?

Mini Quiz

Faced with the chance to speak in front of a large audience, would you:

a) Turn it down. It's your absolute worst nightmare.

b) Muster up the courage.

c) Welcome the opportunity.

If you had to teach a high school class for an hour, what subject would you choose to teach and how would you begin your lesson?

Do you believe the devil is real? If not, what are your thoughts about evil? Does it exist?

When was the last time you really pushed your physical self to the limit? What were you doing and how did you feel before, during, and after?

In relationships, are you more likely to be the heart-breaker or the heart-broken? Why do you think that is?

If you could change your occupation, what would it be? Why aren't you doing it?

What's the best surprise you ever got?

If you could put on an invisible cloak, where would you go and what would you do?

What dish do you love to cook? Why is it your fave, and when and how did you learn it?

What do you say to those annoying telemarketers before hanging up?

Do it! Read your favorite childhood fairy tale to your partner.

What are five situations in which
you would feel really shy?

★

What annoys you most about
the opposite sex?

★

Beards: Cool or ridiculous?

★

Who is the greatest leader of all time?
What makes that person so admirable?

★

What color describes your usual mood?

The handyman you hired didn't do the job quite right. How do you feel about telling him to redo it?

a) Uncomfortable. You'd rather just do it yourself than ask him to fix it.

b) Okay. You know how to ask for changes without being a jerk about it.

c) Fine. Giving directions is second nature to you.

Would you be willing to give up sex for three months if you knew you would be guaranteed super-hot erotic dreams instead?

What are five of your daily rituals (include things like brushing your teeth)?

What do you think is the biggest issue facing this country? What, if anything, have you done to try and improve the problem?

———⭐

Have you ever had a long-distance romance? If so, what were the plusses? What were the minuses?

———⭐

What's the closest call you've had with death? Describe what happened then and how you feel about it now.

Describe the time you met someone and immediately felt connected. Are you still in touch? And is the relationship still as intense?

Are you a collector? If so, what do you collect? If not, what do think is the motivation behind accumulating stuff?

Do it! Plant a tree together, or if you're city dwellers, buy a plant and share the responsibility in caring for it.

What's your treatment for healing a broken heart?

Is there something you once did or
said that is still bothering you?

———★

What's your usual M.O. for
breaking off a relationship?

———★

If you could dial into a "dream machine"
and choose your nocturnal wanderings,
what would you want to dream?

———★

Who's your most eccentric relative?
Describe a few of his or her antics.

Mini Quiz

Is it more important to be:

   a) Honest.

   b) Kind.

   c) Correct.

Nature or nurture? What do you think?

Can you name five unforgivable actions?

Would you lend friends money?

During what period in your life (childhood, high school, college, adulthood) did you meet most of your closest friends?

What was the biggest news event in your life so far? Where were you when you heard about it, or did you experience it first-hand?

Do it! Share your favorite joke.

What do you think of people who spend much of their day working on their laptops while sitting in a café?

When you come up against rules that you personally feel are ridiculous or unfair, do you stick to them anyway?

Can you name five everyday things that make you happy?

Have you ever tracked down an old friend online? What happened after you connected?

Do you shop only when you need something or do you think of it as retail therapy?

How long does it take you to truly
trust someone? Can you explain?

Would you say you're a lucky person?
Give examples of why or why not.

Do you think you could live on a commune
with very little privacy, or do you crave
your own space and alone time?

Mini Quiz

Imagine your political party is running an oaf in the next election. You:

a) Cast your vote for the dummy anyway.

b) Don't vote.

c) Vote for the other candidate.

Would you say you usually offer more praise than criticism? Is that how you were raised?

What was the most tedious movie you've ever seen and what made it so boring?

What grade (A through F) would
you give your parents for their skill
set in raising you? Explain.

★

What news bulletin would
make you very happy?

★

Do you believe in UFOs or life
beyond our own universe?

★

Can you name three bad habits
you'd like to break?

What time in your life would you
say was the least stressed?

Do you believe animals have souls
or consciousness much like us?

Have you ever been ruthlessly teased?
If yes, about what? If not, have you
ever been a bit of a bully?

Do you believe we have free will?

What's the worst job you ever
had? Why was it so terrible?

If you start panicking, what do you
do or tell yourself to calm down?

Do you have an easy or a difficult time
multi-tasking? Can you stick to only one
chore without getting distracted?

Do it! Take turns feeding each other
from a single bowl of ice cream.

How do you feel about guns?

Do you think there are times when stealing is appropriate?

What do you think of Edward Snowden? Hero or enemy of the people? Explain.

Would you be willing to spend a night alone in a house that people have said was haunted?

Given your choice, would you rather
play a game with someone who was
more skilled than you, equally skilled, or
less skilled? What's your reasoning?

———— ⭐

How afraid of dying are you? What
do you imagine happens?

———— ⭐

If you were given ten acres of land,
where would you want it to be and
what would you want to do with it?

What was the worst injury you
got as a child or teenager?

★

Can you describe a time when you really
felt like you were in mortal danger?

★

Mini Quiz

Which of these skin sensations sounds the most
scintillating:

a) Having your body massaged with scented
oils.

b) Jumping into a freezing lake after unwinding
in a mega-hot sauna.

c) Sinking into sun baked beach sand and
having the ocean wash over your legs.

Have you accidentally broken something that was valuable? Did it belong to you or someone else? Did you end up replacing it?

Would you rather make love in the dark, by candlelight, or in natural light?

What steps do you take to protect your privacy on the Internet?

Have you ever read a self-help book that really helped you?

Do it! Try something challenging that neither of you has done before, like jumping on a giant trampoline, zip gliding, or swinging on a trapeze.

Would you rather throw a party or have a party thrown for you? Why?

Do you think it's better to be the one who is loved more or the one who loves more? Why?

Which art form do you enjoy doing more—writing, drawing, or making music? Would you share it publicly?

—⭐

If you could wave a magic wand and uninvent something that already exists, what object would you choose? How do you think it would change the world?

—⭐

When you're traveling, either on a plane, bus, or train, are you likely to strike up a conversation with your seatmate? Or do you avoid making contact?

Do you remember a time you felt so sick you thought you were dying?

What tempts you most but you can usually successfully resist?

Mini Quiz

How would you rate your dance fever?

a) Cool. You don't have much interest in it, but you'll boogie every now and then.

b) Warm. You like it mainly because it's a turn-on.

c) Hot. Whenever you hear the beat, you start moving.

Would you prefer to travel around the country or overseas? What's your thinking?

Would you prefer to travel around the country or overseas? What's your thinking?

How often do you tell little white lies? Do you remember the last one you told?

What is one thing you learned yesterday?

Who is the most challenging person you know?

Do it! Write a poem for each other.

How would you define the concept of "sin"?

What's something you thought you would get
done today, but didn't get around to doing?

Is it difficult for you to spend time
alone or is it something you prefer?

How do you explain the cycle
of birth and death?

Is ignorance bliss? If yes,
why? If no, why not?

What was the most dangerous situation
you were ever in? How did you react?
And do you think you have PTSD from it?

Can you define "true love"?

What does the expression "still waters run deep" mean? And do you think it's true?

Do you think it's better to live in one place or to move around?

Do you always rely on your GPS, or do you usually trust your own sense of direction when driving?

What is your mobile ring tone? Why did you choose it? How often do you change it?

Mini Quiz

At the end of your work day, do you usually feel:

    a) Happy and satisfied.

    b) Glad that you can go out and have fun.

    c) Exhausted and desperate to de-stress and relax.

Are you more concerned with your weight, your finances, or your sexual prowess? What are you doing to improve in this area?

Do you feel poised for a change or pretty much steady with your pedal to the metal?

Do you consider yourself to be a visionary?
If so, in what ways? If not, are you more
likely to rely on someone else's view?
If so, who is this person, and what
does he or she have that you don't?

Are you more likely to make excuses in
order to get out of appointments or do
you stick to honesty as a general rule?

In what ways do you think men and
women communicate differently?

How much confidence do you have in the conventional medical establishment?

━ ⭐

What do you think the planet needs most now—hope, peace, faith, or something else? Can you explain?

━ ⭐

Describe your childhood family dinners. Was the family together on most evenings? Did you sit in the same seat every night? What sort of discussions (if any) did you have? Was it usually peaceful or contentious?

Do you think you're too hard on yourself?
Or too easy? In what ways?

—— ⭐

Do you believe you waste too much
time? If so, in what ways? If not,
how do you honor your time?

—— ⭐

In what ways do you think you're
dishonest with yourself?

Mini Quiz

If you suddenly inherited a large sum of money, you would:

a) Quit your job and see the world.

b) Take up some kind of work that you've always wanted to do even though it doesn't pay much.

c) Continue what you're doing. You love your career.

Who's the most important person in your life right now?

Are you more likely to confide your troubles and fears or do you usually keep those kinds of things to yourself?

In what ways would you like your relationship
to be like your parents', and in what ways
would you definitely want it to be different?

Have you ever considered killing yourself,
even if it was just a momentary thought?
What triggered such a consideration
as brief as it might have been?

Do it! Play a classic board game like
chess, checkers, Scrabble, or Monopoly.

What about your childhood
do you most miss?

Are you for or against fracking?
Why? Why not?

—★

Do you frequently judge others?
Why do you think you do and how
is it affecting your relationships?

—★

Would you rather donate your time or
your money to a worthy cause? Which
do you think is more valuable?

Mini Quiz

For your birthday, would you rather have:

a) Amnesia.

b) Dinner in your favorite restaurant with your loved one or family.

c) A surprise party thrown in your honor.

What would make you stand up and cheer?

Have you experienced unrequited love? What did you learn from it?

Which trait do you believe attracts others to you the most: intellect, looks, or sense of humor?

⭐

Can you name five things about this country that you think are terrific? And five things that you believe need to be changed?

⭐

Would you go to a séance to contact someone you lost? Do you really believe it's possible or are you doing it just out of curiosity?

Do you prefer texting, calling, or emailing for communication? Why?

⸺ ★

If you could read anyone's mind, whose would you choose and why?

⸺ ★

Mini Quiz

Fantasies often take flight before a plane's liftoff. While boarding, you usually think about:

a) Gliding gently onto the runway of your destination.

b) A terrorist takeover or crash landing.

c) Sitting next to an interesting stranger.

Let's say you get a second chance
on your life. What is the first
thing you would do over?

⭐

What do you think is the most horrible
sound in the world? The sweetest?

⭐

How do you feel about
nostalgia? Good or bad?

⭐

What would someone have to do
in order for you to ask him or her to
leave a party you were hosting?

Do it! Read the same book.

What was the last thing that happened
to make you want to scream out loud
(even though you kept your cool)?

What do you usually do when
you can't sleep at night?

What's the first thing that comes to mind
when you hear the word "unjust"?

What's the most disgusting food
you've ever eaten—or tried to eat?

★

Can you describe a vacation that
was anything but relaxing?

★

Who is the happiest person you
know? Describe the way he or she
expresses an upbeat attitude.

★

Can you name five personality traits that
would turn you off a prospective partner?
Which do you find the most offensive?

Mini Quiz

If someone broke a promise made to you, would you most likely:

a) Bring their attention to it right then and there.

b) Be pissed in the moment, but let it go.

c) Be angry and carry a grudge for a while.

Do you usually overpack or underpack for a trip?

Do it! Make a playlist of your favorite romantic songs.

What is a personal accomplishment
that you're especially proud of?

★

If you were to write a Wikipedia entry,
what subject would you choose?

★

Which do you think is unhealthier, marijuana
or alcohol? Explain your position.

★

Approximately how many books a
year do you read? What was the
title of your most recent favorite and
why did you like it so much?

Is there any place on somebody's body where a tattoo or piercing would really gross you out?

What would you like to do with your partner that you've never done before?

Mini Quiz

The health food section of the store is offering some rather expensive goodies. You're more likely to:

a) Treat yourself and buy the tastiest item.

b) Make do with a few samples.

c) Walk by—you don't like to play with temptation.

Do you think monogamy is really possible?
Do you think it's necessary in order to
keep a relationship intimate and solid?

★

What five things do you think you should
take less seriously? What five things do
you think you should take more seriously?

★

What do you think about the
power of eye contact?

★

Do it! Make out for ten minutes.

If you had to make a choice between being super-healthy and super-hot, which would you choose and why?

How do you think drunk drivers who cause serious injuries or death should be punished? What's your reasoning?

If you were given ten minutes to spend with the president of the United States, what would you want to talk about?

What acts of kindness were shown to you that you won't ever forget?

Do you think really rich people are happier? Why or why not?

★

Can you name five things you dislike about committed relationships? And five things you enjoy?

★

Do you think your partner truly trusts you? Why or why not?

★

What's a good habit that if you could, you would develop starting today?

Can you think of a circumstance that
would lead you to betray a friend?

What's the biggest skeleton
in your family's closet?

Would you say you're a pretty
predictable person, or do you tend to
be unpredictable? Offer an example.

Name three things that you feel you're
too old to do, and explain why.

Mini Quiz

If you were in the mood for a leisurely drive, where would you head?

a) Down a country road.

b) Around town.

c) To the shopping mall.

Do you believe in capital punishment? Why or why not?

How important is weather to you? For example, would a rainy day stop you from strolling on the beach or a super-warm day prevent you from taking a hike?

Would you rescue a dog from the pound that was on death row even though you weren't planning on getting a pet?

——⭐

Do it! Have a thumb war.

——⭐

Do you think jealousy can be a healthy reaction or is it always destructive? Do you consider yourself a jealous person?

——⭐

Ever had a threesome? Or thought about it?

What about competitiveness?
Good or bad? Do you consider
yourself a competitive person?

Did you ever overreact because of a
misunderstanding on your end? What was it
about? How did you make amends, or did
you let it go without explanation or apology?

Has someone ever sworn you to
secrecy, but either by accident or
on purpose, you blabbed?

Have you ever been punked?
When and how?

Do you consider yourself to be an open book
or are you pretty tough to get to know?

Do you think all human beings basically
want the same things in life?

What does the expression "charity
begins at home" mean to you?

What's your debt situation? If you don't have any, what's your budgeting secret? If you have debt, is it enough to keep you up at night, and what's your plan, if any, to deal with it?

In your opinion which is more of a virtue: kindness or honesty? Explain.

What do you think about opiate addiction? Is it the fault of the pharmaceutical industry or human weakness?

Do it! Tickle each other until
someone cries "Uncle!"

★

What's your definition of "spiritual"?
Is that how you see yourself?

★

Do you binge watch without guilt?

★

Who would you most likely
buy an impulse gift for?

Mini Quiz

If you were at a dinner party and found yourself disagreeing with your host's view, you would probably:

a) Still stress your view.

b) Keep the conversation pleasant, even if it means conceding.

c) Politely smile and nod but inwardly seethe.

When you're out for lunch with friends, are you more likely to pay your portion, split the bill evenly, or pick up the entire tab?

What's your ideal leisurely Sunday afternoon?

Do you believe in the practice of positive affirmations? If so, what are a few that you might tell yourself?

Do you have a strong preference for whether you're holding the steering wheel or sitting in the passenger's seat? Which is it and what's your thinking?

Where's the strangest place you had sex?

Are you a thrill seeker? For example, do you opt for scary amusement park rides, ski the black diamond, mountain climb, ride motorcycles, etc.?

Are you more of an apologizer or do you tend to make excuses? Describe one time today or yesterday when you used either approach.

How can partners prevent themselves from becoming totally codependent? Offer four of your favorite tips.

Who's the best cook you know,
and what's their best dish?

What's the most common compliment you
receive? And what's your usual response?

You know the expression: To err is human
and to forgive is divine. Do you believe
any mistake has the potential to be
forgiven? What was the most difficult
time you had to conjure forgiveness?

Would you be willing to do anything
to save your relationship? Where
would you draw the line?

★

What are your thoughts about palm reading?

★

Do it! Watch the sunrise or sunset together.

★

Do you prefer friends to text first before
calling to see if it's a good time to
talk? Or would you rather just ignore
the call when you're busy? Or interrupt
what you're doing and take it?

Around how many times a day
do you look in the mirror?

How often do you experience the blues?

Do you remember the day you
first met your partner?

Would you rather ask questions
or trust your instincts?

When it comes to making love, would you describe yourself as the:

   a) Initiator.

   b) Mentor.

   c) Follower.

Can you name five things you
hate spending money on?

What other country would you
like to live in for one year?

Are you more likely to be sarcastic or ironic?

On a scale of one to ten, how sociable
are you? Would you like to increase
or decrease that number—or are you
happy with your level of sociability?

Have you ever covertly read another
person's texts or emails? What was the
circumstance that drove you to do it?

Do you have an idea for a
startup? Or an invention?

When you're apart from your partner, how
often do you think about him or her?

What's your opinion about sleeping in separate beds? Is it ever a good idea or is it the road to romantic ruin?

If you could trade places with anyone for a day, who would you choose?

Do you trust your partner to always tell the truth?

Would you want to live beyond a hundred years? Why or why not?

If you could afford either a cook, masseur, chauffeur, maid, or fitness trainer, who would you hire?

How is the paper money in your wallet arranged? In the same vein, what do you think about the philosophy that contends respecting your money (even in this way) means you'll acquire more?

Hey, is money the root of all that's evil?

Has anyone ever accidentally seen you naked?

Mini Quiz

If your partner asked whether you liked a shirt he or she was wearing and you didn't, would you probably:

a) Tell the honest truth so it won't be worn again.

b) Sugarcoat your opinion by stressing the positive.

c) Offer a white lie and say, "You look great!"

When speaking with people in authority are you usually more anxious or defiant?

Do you think you're sort of lazy?

Would you rather spend the day with someone who liked to engage in big philosophical issues or someone who just wanted to hang out and have fun?

Do it! Raise a glass and make a toast to your partner.

If you had to give up either sweet or spicy foods, which would you choose? And how much of a sacrifice would it be?

Do you think you say "I love you" too often or not often enough? Why is that?

If your partner said something
that wasn't true in front of another
couple, what would you do?

⭐

What's more important to you: the way
your lover smells or the way they feel?

⭐

How would you describe your face?

⭐

Do you have a childhood nickname that only
a few people use now? Who are those folks?

What do you think are the special
abilities that make an expert flirt?

When you're having an argument,
do you find yourself focusing more
on getting your opinion across or
keeping the situation under control?

Do you think pride is a good
thing? Why or why not?

Were you a cool kid when you were
growing up or more of a geek or nerd?

What's the worst travel
experience you ever had?

★

What are you most ashamed of?

★

Who is someone you wish you never met?

★

What would you like to do on
a rainy Sunday afternoon?

Mini Quiz

If the person ahead of you on the supermarket express aisle had many more than the items allotted, would you:

a) Suggest he or she move to a regular line.

b) Say nothing.

c) Go to another line.

What do you consider your greatest accomplishment?

What would you do if you discovered a close relative was addicted to heroin or another drug?

Do you remember a nightmare
medical experience?

⎯⎯★

Do you sometimes get paranoid that
you're going to lose your job?

⎯⎯★

Do you think tidiness is a sign that
a person isn't creative? Or is it an
indication of competence?

⎯⎯★

What are three things you feel
absolutely neutral about?

If you wrote a book, whom would you name in the dedication?

⭐

Do you remember the last time you cried?

⭐

Everything happens for a reason. Why do you think you met your partner?

⭐

What was the best party you ever went to?

⭐

Who was the most inspiring teacher you ever had?

Do it! Work out together.

— ★

If you were unsure of how to solve a problem, would you "sleep on it"?

— ★

What act could you perform in a circus?

— ★

What recent tragic news story touched you the deepest?

— ★

Would you accept a dare? Where might you draw the line?

What is (or would be) your Twitter username?

Would you be more likely to place a bet
at a poker table or buy a lottery ticket?

Would you still want to be with your partner
if he or she looked completely different?

How would you be likely to react if
someone spilled wine on your lap?

Do you speak to strangers in elevators?

Are you a dedicated recycler?

⭐

Do you pick your nose?

⭐

What's your definition of a narcissist?

⭐

Should a television be kept in the bedroom?

⭐

Would you rather read a book
or play a video game?

What's your favorite work of art?

When you travel, do you prefer
to settle in one place, or explore
several different locations?

Do you prefer a hot climate
or a cold climate?

How many friends do you have
outside of your own race?

Do you enjoy spending time with children?

★

When you enter a home where
artificially scented products are
used, are you sensitive to it?

★

When was the last time you cleaned
the inside of your kitchen trash bin?

★

Do you correct people's grammar
or pronunciation?

What are two things you feel
competent to teach others?

Are you an interrupter?

Have you ever stolen a coworker's
idea and taken credit for it? Or
has that happened to you?

Do you do your own taxes?

Can you operate a power tool?

Are you able to control your
thoughts much of the time?

Do you dress to express yourself,
or do you dress to blend in?

Would you tell someone you loved him or her
if you'd only known the person for a week?

Have you ever posed nude?

Do you believe self-improvement
is an ongoing process?

Would you rather cook or clean?

—★

Could you help with an assisted suicide for
somebody who is terminally ill and in pain?

—★

How comfortable are you
around very old people?

—★

Are you more of a sports
spectator or a participant?

—★

Do you write poetry?

Do you have more in assets
than you owe in debt?

★

Were you big "trouble" as a teenager?

★

How do you react to know-it-alls?

★

Have you ever spread a rumor?

★

Do you know any magic tricks?

Would you twerk?

———⭐

Do you usually get your shoes
repaired or do you discard them?

———⭐

Do it! Offer a foot massage.

———⭐

Have you ever stomped out
of a room in anger?

———⭐

How do you feel about clowns?

Would you go to a foreign film?

Are you more of a penny pincher or someone who spends freely?

How often do you see your extended family?

Would you go to Burning Man?

Do you enjoy camping out?

Would you say you were born
in the wrong decade?

On average, how much time do
you spend grooming before leaving
your house in the morning?

Have you ever worked for a political
candidate or spoken strongly
about one you supported?

Does it matter to you if a room
has fluorescent lighting?

How many pictures of yourself do you
have displayed in your home?

Would you enter a dance contest?

What sparks your competitive spirit?

Do you let your gas tank reach "E" frequently
or are you more likely to be sure to have
at least a quarter of the tank filled?

When you're not feeling well, do you
prefer to be fussed over or left alone?

Mini Quiz

If you were served cool soup or coffee at a restaurant, would you be more likely to:

a) Send it back.

b) Leave it untouched.

c) Drink it anyway.

What was your best subject in high school? Are you still interested in it?

How often do you look at your photos either on your mobile phone or computer? And how often do you change your screensavers?

If you had to let just one person know
your every feeling and every thought
for a day, who would you choose
that person to be? And why?

———★

When you hear about yet another
mass shooting, what is usually your
first reaction? Your second?

———★

If you're an overnight guest at someone's
house, would you be more likely to offer to
cook, buy something for dinner (including
alcohol), or take your host out for a meal?

What would you do (or say) if
someone insulted your partner when
he or she wasn't present?

What's the very first memory you can recall?

Have you ever witnessed a violent act such
as a physical fight, robbery, or murder?

Why do you think so many
Americans have drug problems?

What was the absolute worst sexual
experience you had in your life?

⭐

What would you do if you felt as if your
best friend was pulling away from you?

⭐

Can you share your usual weekday
routine from the time you wake
up to the time you tuck in?

⭐

Do it! Compose a love letter.

Have you ever performed in a talent show? What was your act?

How do you imagine a close brush with death would change you?

Mini Quiz

Are you more likely to be envious of another's:

a) Physical appearance.

b) Career accomplishments.

c) Stuff.

What's the worst investment you
ever made? The best?

★

What do you think is particularly admirable
about the younger generation?

★

What book had the biggest impact on you?

★

What's your favorite animated
movie of all time?

★

Manicure or pedicure?

What are four qualities you most
admire in your best friend?

How would you feel about your partner
going on a month-long holiday without you?

Let's say you could safely grab
five things from a burning house.
What would those items be?

Can you describe a situation that brings
out your feelings of insecurity?

What are three ways men are
discriminated against?

⎯⎯⎯ ★

What are three ways women
are discriminated against?

⎯⎯⎯ ★

Mini Quiz

What's the first question you ask yourself when
choosing something to wear for a business event?

a) Is it comfortable?

b) Does it make me look powerful?

c) Is it appropriate for the situation?

What could a friend do that under no circumstances would you be able to forgive?

If you knew someone who was a complete "sponge" and always taking, taking, taking but never giving, could you still be friends? Why or why not?

How often do you weigh yourself? If it's frequently, does it affect your eating choices?

What are two things you won't leave your home without?

You're working under a tight work deadline and every minute counts when your friend calls with a problem that needs to be solved immediately. Do you stop what you're doing? Why or why not?

———⭐

What do you think the saying "Smile and the world smiles with you" means?

———⭐

If you saw a stranger littering, would you say something, pick up the discarded trash and put it in a bin, or more likely just walk by?

———⭐

Do you usually drive the speed limit, over the speed limit, or slightly under?

Would you pick up a hitchhiker?
What's your reasoning?

What is your least favorite
dessert? Your favorite? Is there any
sweet you just won't eat?

What would you do if someone
were talking in a movie theater and
disturbing your experience, as well as
probably others in the audience?

Where do you stand on gun control?

Do you have a packed bag in case of an emergency? If so, what's in it? If not, do you ever think about creating one—or do you feel it's a waste of time and effort?

— ★

What are three jobs you definitely couldn't do?

— ★

Do you remember a time when you were disappointed because you weren't chosen for something?

— ★

What's your dieting philosophy?

If you were lost, would you ask a stranger for directions, or would you rather spend time figuring out where to go, trusting you'll eventually get to your destination?

Would you rather hike up a steep mountain, walk through a dessert, or swim across a big lake?

Other than buying food, do you do more of your purchasing over the Internet or in brick-and-mortar stores?

What do you think about boycotting a product if you disagree with its company's policies? Have you ever done it?

— ★

What's your thinking on the transgender bathroom issue?

— ★

Do you prefer to wear solids or prints (including plaids)?

— ★

Who do you think was the best president, alive or dead? Why? And who was the worst?

Would rather dance to a live band, a professional DJ, or your own playlist?

— ★

Which spectator sport would you enjoy seeing the most?

— ★

Can you remember a time in your childhood when you felt as if you were in danger?

— ★

If someone was pursuing you romantically but you couldn't care less, how would you communicate your disinterest?

What kind of volunteer work
would you choose to do?

Do you think you have a healthy
body image? In what ways yes and
in what ways not so much?

Are you someone who easily burns
bridges? Or are you more into
repairing the damage done?

Would you risk your life to save an animal?

How do you feel about Valentine's Day? An opportunity to express love and appreciation or a commercial holiday created by companies to make money?

Would you walk or ride a bike to raise funds for a charity if it means you have to ask friends and acquaintances to make a donation in your support?

Could you live with a roommate at this time in your life?

Are you close friends with anyone who has completely different political views than you?

— ★

Do you curse a lot? A little? Not at all?

— ★

What's your opinion of
Kickstarter campaigns?

— ★

How would you describe your handshake?
Strong? Firm? Warm? Soft?

Mini Quiz

Which of these behaviors do you think offers the most memorable impression when interviewing for a job?

a) Making frequent eye contact and smiling when speaking.

b) Asking insightful questions, including one personal question about the interviewer.

c) Following up with a phone call or sending a thank you email.

On an average day, how much time do you spend in bed?

Do you prefer to work in silence or with music in the background?

Do you think you're more motivated
by achievement or recognition?
Can you give an example?

If your partner was gaining a lot of weight
and you were concerned for health reasons,
how would you approach the subject?

How much do you worry about
what people think of you?

What are you usually doing
on Saturday mornings?

Are you more of a collaborator or an
independent creator? Can you give
an example of the last time you either
took the lead or joined others?

Which game of chance would
you most enjoy playing? When
was the last time you did it?

Who would you rely on more for advice—an
astrologer, psychologist, or good friend?

How would you describe your handwriting?

Mini Quiz

You're planning to tackle a big project when something fun comes up. You:

a) Reschedule your project and have fun.

b) Get at least half done, then leave.

c) Finish the project completely before you go out.

How do you feel about unexpected guests showing up at your door?

On the whole, what do you think about our justice system?

Would you rather have your desk facing a window, door, or wall—and why?

⎯ ★

What quality do you think is most important in a friend: shared values, reliability, or an upbeat outlook?

⎯ ★

Have you ever had a premonition that came true?

⎯ ★

What are usually the first thoughts that come to you when you wake in the morning?

Do it! Mirror gaze. Standing in front
of the same mirror, stare at each
other's reflection for a few minutes.

———⋆

What do you think is the likelihood that
a couple who breaks up and gets back
together will have a lasting relationship?

———⋆

Mini Quiz

Which of these reality shows would you be most
likely to watch?

a) The Bachelor or The Bachelorette

b) Keeping Up with the Kardashians

c) The Voice

Do you usually go back to the same place for vacations or research and try something new?

When there are mass shootings, is your first reaction usually to blame the gun industry, our mental health system, or the existence of evil? Explain your reasoning.

When was the last time you bought an article of clothing?

What was the worst storm or other natural disaster you experienced?

When you were growing up, what remedy did your mother offer for the common cold? Do you still use it today?

What's your take on vegan diets?

Mini Quiz

If stuck in traffic, you'd be most likely to:

a) Strategize another way to get where you're going.

b) Look for a better lane and hope the traffic cleared up soon.

c) Put on your favorite music or talk show and relax.

Shuffleboard or ping-pong?

What are three must-dos for
a relationship to work?

What meal do you enjoy most?

Would you fake an orgasm?

How much attention do you
pay to your posture?

Do you get choked up at weddings?

Ⓐ

For dessert, would you be more
likely to order a selection of fruits,
cheeses, cookies, or sorbets?

Ⓐ

Who's the most authentically
spiritual person you know?

Ⓐ

How would you say the world
has changed since 9/11?

What's the most serious injury
you've ever suffered?

Would you rather visit India or China?

What's the most romantic date you ever had?

Would most of your friends describe
you as self-confident or humble?

What's the best way to earn
a person's respect?

Who's your favorite comedian?

★

Do It! Draw a heart on the bathroom
mirror for your partner.

★

If you were going to sign up for a class
with your partner, what would you take?

★

If you could change one thing about
the way you look, what would it be?

★

Do you try to overcome negative self-
talk? If so, what techniques do you use?

Using only one sentence, can
you describe yourself?

What are three loathsome chores?

How important is it to you that
people remember, pronounce, and
spell your name correctly?

What are two pieces of advice
you would give to all parents?

What's your definition of peace?

Do you believe the opposite sex communicates differently? In what ways?

★

When do you feel the loneliest?

★

Have you ever been physically, sexually, or emotionally abused?

★

What's your favorite place on earth?

Do you think we live the life we imagine?

Have you encountered someone recently
who just rubbed you the wrong way?

If you could hire a decorator for
the day, what room in your home
would you want redone?

If money doesn't bring
happiness, what does?

Can you give an example of wisdom
as opposed to intelligence?

★

What's the best way to earn a partner's trust?

★

Describe your thinking around natural
remedies. Effective or bogus?

★

What's your feeling about one-night stands?

★

Where do you see yourself
five years from now?

Who's more important in your life: friends or family?

Would you move a great distance for a job?

What do you think about polyamory (open relationships)?

How important do you think physical attractiveness is in a relationship?

What was the first impression
you had of me?

In your opinion, does size matter?

What is the most expensive
gift you've ever given?

Have you ever said "I love you" when you
didn't mean it? What was the circumstance?

Have you ever driven drunk?
How often? Ever gotten a ticket
or gotten into an accident?

Do you like my friends? Who do you
like the most? The least? Why?

What's one word you would
use to describe yourself?

How old were you when you went on
your first date? Where did you go?
Did you have any kind of sex?

Who was your hero when you were a kid?

★

Imagine your best friend warns you that
I'm bad news. What would you do?

★

What were your high school days like?

★

Do it! Challenge each other to a trivia match.

★

Are you more a dog person or a cat person?

What are two quirky things
about me that you like?

In an ideal world, how often
would we have sex?

Do you believe opposites attract?
How do you think we're different?
How are we the same?

Would you tell me if I had bad
breath, a piece of food on my face,
or snot sticking out of my nose?

Are you into playful S&M, including
a little light bondage?

Can you name three things I do or say
that make you feel especially loved?

What scares you the most
about our relationship?

If money weren't an issue, what
would you be doing right now?

What holidays do you enjoy
celebrating, if any?

Do you think experiences with
exes help or hinder us?

Would you be willing to bail me out if I
had crushing debt? Do you have a limit?

Do you believe in spending money on
life insurance? What's your reasoning?

Would you want to travel to another planet?

Have you ever had a crush on a teacher?

How important is having children to you?

What's the best romantic advice you've
ever gotten? What would be the best
romantic advice you could give?

Do you like to talk dirty or hear
dirty talk? Or is it a turn-off?

Try reading my mind. What am I thinking right in this second?

Do you think some things are unforgivable? Like what?

Plans for the evening: Would you rather choose or have your partner do it? How come?

What would be your ideal ticket for president and vice president? What's your thinking behind it?

What's your opinion about May-December relationships? Cougars?

⭐

Is it possible to be too nice?

⭐

If you had an entire day to spend at a beach resort, describe what you would do. Drink cocktails? Read in a chair? Ride the waves? Walk along the sand?

⭐

How important is it to remember names of people you meet? Do you remember a time when you blanked on an important intro?

What was the grossest thing you ever did?

★

What would you think about someone
who had to compromise his or her values
in order to achieve something great?

★

Let's say you're enjoying a dinner party
at a friend's house and you find several
hairs in your soup. What would you do?

★

Do you give to people who beg for money?
If so, how often? What's your reasoning?

Is it difficult to say no if someone
asks you for a favor?

Have you ever hung up or come very close to
hanging up on someone because you were
so angry? What were the circumstances?

What's too serious to be joked about?

Do it! Share an extremely ripe fruit like a
peach, plum, or strawberry with your partner.

Do you think everyone should have
to carry personal ID all the time?

If all your neighbors owned guns, would
you feel more protected or less safe?

If you could plan how you were going
to die, what way would it be?

Would you embark on a passionate
love affair if you knew down the road it
would definitely end in heartbreak?

If you could plan how you were going
to die, what way would it be?

Let's say you were in charge of putting the likeness of a famous person on the ten dollar bill. Who would you choose?

———⭐

Can you recall the last time you blurted out something you ended up regretting?

———⭐

Mini Quiz

On an average day, do you apologize to your partner:

a) Once or twice, if at all.

b) About five times.

c) Between six and a dozen times.

Do you consider yourself to be
a dreamer or a realist?

If you had to give up either your
sense of sight, sound, or touch,
which one would you choose?

If you weren't able to erase your online
history, how would it affect your Internet use?

How do you define the word "lovely"?

Do it! Rap a love song.

— ★

If someone went rummaging through
your closet or drawers, what would
be the most shocking, or at least
surprising, thing they would find?

— ★

Do you think we should negotiate with
terrorists in order to save hostages' lives?

— ★

What's the most valuable thing you've
taken that wasn't really yours?

What are three of the worst things
about being your gender? The best?

What flaw would be enough
to cause a break-up?

Do it! Give your partner a piggyback ride.

Have you ever masturbated
in a public place?

What's your secret prejudice?

Mini Quiz

If your partner says something hurtful, are you more likely to:

   a) Admit your feelings are hurt.

   b) Offer a cold shoulder until your feelings heal.

   c) Simply hope it doesn't happen again.

What makes you feel the most insecure?

Would you still get married if your future spouse went blind?

What television show do you watch that you're a little embarrassed about?

What's your biggest sin?

Can you recall a time when
you lost your dignity?

What was the last intimate moment you
ruined? And how did you do it?

What haven't you done sexually
that you dream about doing?

What do you often think about
when you're alone in your car?

— ★

If you could make a law that's not already
on the books, what would it be?

— ★

What's the greatest accomplishment
of your life so far?

— ★

Have you ever slapped anyone?
What were the circumstances?

Mini Quiz

Which of these statements best describes how up-to-the-minute your partner is on your life?

a) On the same page.

b) Somewhere in the chapter.

c) Rarely, if ever, opens the book.

What's the difference between
having sex and making love?

Can you name something you're glad
you'll never have to do again?

Define "truth."

What's your pet peeve?

Does spending time with others usually
energize you or drain you?

If you could write a note to your younger
self offering advice, what would it be?

Do you think social media brings us closer together or isolates us more?

If you witnessed someone spanking a child, would you say or do anything to try and stop it?

Do you believe the basic nature of humans is kindness? Give examples either way.

Is it easy or difficult for you to change your mind? Describe a time when it was difficult.

Do you think the media
controls public opinion?

What three interests do you share with
your colleagues or fellow students?

Can you recall a particularly memorable
summer vacation when you were a kid?

What signals do you think your
body language is sending out?

ACKNOWLEDGMENTS

I'd like to thank the extraordinary Ulysses family with special appreciation to Bridget Thoreson, Kourtney Joy, Lauren Harrison, and Juana Castro. Gratitude to my awesome son, Gabe, and his heart center, Ariel, as well as to all my friends who ask thoughtful questions and, in those times when I'm floundering, offer just the right answers.

ABOUT THE AUTHOR

Robin Westen has authored over a dozen books, including *Relationship Repair* and *V Is for Vagina* (coauthored with Dr. Alyssa Dweck), and has contributed to *Mr. Wrong: Real Life Tales of the Men We Used to Love*. She was an Emmy award-winning writer for the ABC television show *FYI*, a sex advice columnist for *Woman's Own Magazine*, and she also wrote a weekly pop psychology quiz for *Woman's World Magazine* for more than 18 years. A collection of her columns was published in two volumes: *The Big Book of Personality Tests for Women: 100 Fun-to-Take, Easy-to-Score Quizzes That Reveal Your Hidden Potential in Life, Love and Work*, and *The Big Book of Relationship Quizzes: 100 Tests and Quizzes to Let You Know Who's Who in Your Life*. She splits her time between Brooklyn and Vermont.